HELP FOR THE HELP...MEET

When the Helper Needs Help

DR. CYNTHIA MCINNIS

Help for the Help...Meet
When the Helper Needs Help

Printed in the United States of America First Printing, 2023

ISBN: 978-1-7338592-6-4

BALM2 Productions, Inc.
Brooklyn, NY

Table of Contents

LESSON ONE
The Will and Purpose of God

And the LORD God said, *It is* **not good** that the man should be alone; **Not good;** not convenient either for my purpose of the increase of mankind, or for man's personal comfort, or for the propagation of his kind. This all-familiar story begins with the very reason for our existence ladies. After God masterfully designed and crafted his most precious commodity, in whom he breathed his very own breath and man became a living soul, he said, "It is NOT good." For the first time in the history of His creative utterances we hear the negative. After having said that everything He created was good, we hear the strange utterance of negativity out of the mouth of God. "It is not good that the man should be alone."

Ladies! We were created to be problem solvers. We were created to turn a negative into a positive. How about that? We were created to help. While the modern-day term, "The help" sends off a slightly negative tone, it is in fact the highest compliment ever to be paid to any human being. Being in the position to help should be the most sought-after position in the world. God did not design us to need the help, but to be the help. When God created you, His intention was clear that you would never have to go outside of Him for help. When we get married, we, in essence, agree to be the help.

I remember once, when I was a new wife and then a new mother, and then a mother again. We had a business, worked full-time jobs and were committed and faithful to ministry. After having been completely exhausted and in the middle of a full-fledged hissy fit, I dropped to the floor and cried out, "Lord, If I'm supposed to be His help, who is going to help me?" Oh! It was one of those coughing and hiccupping cries that lasted entirely too long. After I finally coughed my last cough and hiccupped my last hiccup, the Lord gently spoke to me and said, "Cynthia, you help him and I will help you." I got up from the floor knowing that I had the better deal. Although I was giving it my very best shot and trying to do as much as I could to be the best wife and mother I could have been, my help was limited and frail. The best help that I could give was subject to the limitations of my flesh. But God is faultless and infallible. His help is limitless, and he is ever-present. He is your help. He is your strength. He is your strong tower. He helps you to do what you've been designed to do. (Excerpt from, The Genesis Woman, E-book 2020, McInnis, Cynthia) Before sin entered into the world, Adam had no sinful desires. He had no lusts. He had only the tenacity to do the will of God for which he was created. Because there were no women in existence, he had no desire for a woman.

"I will make him an help meet for him." It was God's idea to make a person that was *meet or suitable* for his man. Making a woman was God's idea. Adam was perfectly content with the will of God for his life. He carried out his assignment as God instructed.

And out of the ground the LORD God formed every beast of the field, and every fowl of the air; and brought *them* unto Adam to see what he would call them: and whatsoever Adam called every living creature, that *was* the name thereof. And Adam gave names to all cattle, and to the fowl of the air, and to every beast of the field; but for Adam there was not found an help meet for him.

And the LORD God caused a deep sleep to fall upon Adam, and he slept: and he took one of his ribs and closed up the flesh instead thereof; And the rib, which the LORD God had taken from man, made he a woman, and brought her unto the man.

She was made from what was taken out of the man and God made her into a woman that would be suitable for His man and convenient for His purpose of the increase of mankind, or for man's personal comfort, or for the propagation of his kind. *A help meet for him —* כנגדו, *chenegdo,* a most significant phrase; one *as before him,* or *correspondent to him,* his counterpart, suitable to his nature and his need, one like himself in shape, constitution, and disposition, *a second self:* one to be at hand, or near to him, to converse familiarly with him, to be always ready to assist and support and comfort him, and whose care and business it should be to please and help him to fulfil his God-given purpose.

God, as her Father, brought the woman to the man, as his second self, and a help meet for him. That wife, who is of God's making by special grace, and of God's bringing by special providence, is likely to prove a help meet for a man. See what need there is, both of prudence and prayer in the choice of this relationship, which is so near and so lasting.

This is the reason the woman was created. There is no mention here of her personal happiness, dreams or desires. If this sounds sad and pitiful to you it is because you are seeing her as you see yourself. Instead, see her as one who simply did not have any of those. She was perfectly fine with the will of God for her life. He then brought her to His man and presented her to Him as a gift, as God's gift to man.

The first voice she would hear upon creation was not the voice of God but the voice of a man, Adam. As was his nature, he did his regular assignment and gave her a name. he recognized that she was like him and had come out of him. He recognized that she was made for him and a gift presented to him so he named her appropriately, a man with a womb. Woman.
And Adam said, "This is now bone of my bones, and flesh of my flesh: she shall be called Woman, because she was taken out of Man." Genesis 2:23

This is the intentional will of God. Therefore, shall a man leave his father and his mother, and shall cleave unto his wife: and they shall be one flesh. And they were both naked, the man and his wife, and were not ashamed. They were not ashamed of anything. They were content to do the will of God for their lives as He intended. This was the state of man and woman before sin. Pause. Ponder that idea for a few moments.

God's Man was not incomplete without a woman, but he was made better by having a woman that was suitable to help him carry out his God-given assignment in the earth. It has been said that the woman completes the man and that the man completes the woman. This would mean that God created them incompletely, needing something else to be complete. This is not possible!

We must understand God to be the perfect creator of all things perfect. Nothing missing. Nothing broken.

She was made for the man, and he brought her unto the man. God created you for his man and gave you to him, as a gift. He made you the perfect gift for his man. Everything his man needed in the earth would come from you. You were designed to be his perfect help. Not his helpmate but help made suitably, appropriately, and perfect for him. Perfect? I guess that word is throwing some of you off kilter right now but please, don't let the word, perfect, throw you. Whenever we get nervous about words like perfect, we are obviously thinking about ourselves and all of our imperfections flash before our eyes. Let us consider that you did not design yourself, but God did. We must know and appreciate the fact that God creates nothing imperfectly. Girl! You are a perfect design. Now, we have to see what happened to change our perceptions of ourselves. Some of us were never told who we are from God's perspective. We never told our own daughters what God thinks about them. We may have told them that they come from the ancestry of Kings and Queens in Mother Africa, or we reminded them of the greatness that runs through the family bloodline. We may have done our best to relate to the inner greatness of some historic past but that is not far enough. I take you back to the day in that garden when God himself made the masterpiece that is you. Your core design is perfect. Everything about you is perfect. We have allowed the circumstances of life; the societal images and the pain of our choices cause us to see something else. Something that we find shame, guilt, or embarrassment with but please let me take you back to the core of who you are. You are God's gift and don't you ever forget that.

Lesson Challenge

Challenge 1.1

Write a paragraph explaining your understanding of God's original purpose for creating a man and His original purpose for creating a woman.

_____

_____

_____

_____

_____

_____

_____

_____

_____

_____

_____

_____

_____

_____

_____

_____

_____

_____

_____

_____

_____

_____

Challenge 1.2
How does this differ from any ideas you may have had prior to acquiring this knowledge?

_____

_____

_____

_____

_____

_____

_____

_____

_____

_____

_____

_____

_____

_____

_____

_____

_____

_____

_____

_____

_____

Challenge 1.3
Does this knowledge cause any change to your expectations of yourself, your spouse, your fellow-man? If so, what are they?

_____

_____

_____

_____

_____

_____

_____

_____

_____

_____

_____

_____

_____

_____

_____

_____

_____

_____

_____

_____

_____

_____

Final Challenge
What do you think is the will of God for your life right now? (I have no idea is an acceptable

answer.)

_____

_____

_____

_____

_____

_____

_____

_____

_____

_____

_____

_____

_____

_____

_____

_____

_____

_____

_____

_____

_____

ADDITIONAL RESOURCE

SCAN THE CODE TO DOWNLOAD

LESSON TWO

Losing Our Focus

Both man and woman are completely perfect alone. However, when we read God's full intention for them in Genesis 1: **27** So God created man in his own image, in the image of God created he him; male and female created he them. **28** And God blessed them, and God said unto them, **Be fruitful, and multiply, and replenish the earth,** and subdue it: and have dominion over the fish of the sea, and over the fowl of the air, and over every living thing that moveth upon the earth. It is here that we see why God said it is not good for the man to be alone. It had little to do with the man, but all to do with the *will* of God for mankind. It is not good for Adam to be alone because alone, he cannot fulfill his purpose in the earth. He cannot procreate alone. He cannot be fruitful and multiply. He cannot replenish the earth, alone.

What is my point? Am I desperately trying to show the insignificance of women? God forbid. I am a woman. I am, however, trying to emphasize God's will and intention as priority in everything He created. Life has somehow caused us to lose focus on God's will and purpose and place more and more emphasis on the wills and purposes for our own lives.

Terms like, "I don't like this. I don't want this. I don't deserve this. I deserve that. I'm not happy. I am not fulfilled. I feel, I feel, I feel", now dominate our cultures, our families, our marriages, and our lives. If things are not our way, our will, we have taken the right to disrupt the plan and purpose of God and manipulate it into what satisfies us the most. God help us.

Adam and Eve were selfless and existed only to fulfill the destiny of God's intention for their lives. They lived in utter peace and pure delight …until sin happened!

Quite naturally, we understand that the state of men and women has gravely changed over the span of time. Sin has introduced so many ideas and cultures that do not resemble the innocence of mankind's original state and are not even remotely close to God's original and intentional will for His creation. Life was simple. Life was easy. Mankind and his God, man and his wife were in a perfect relationship until sin happened.

Something inside of every one of us should yearn for that again! As contradictory as it may sound in this world so filled with *me-ism*, self-indulgence, self-gratification, self-love, selfie-ism and selfishness, this is very much possible again.

Once we master practicing the will of God for our lives as individuals, and form a right relationship with our God, then we can attempt to form meaningful and lasting relationships with others. Most of us have already formed relationships, even marriages, live in families, work on jobs with people long before we even considered the will of God for our lives so we must work backwards, whether those relationships seem fine or not. We must go all the way backwards … back to Eden. Back to God's original intent. Then we must endeavor to live in the will of God for our own lives while we navigate through life with others. Whew! What an incredible task. It seems hard but trust me, it is not as hard as it seems.

Life in God's will is an easy life, it is the way of those who transgress against the will of God that is hard. **Proverbs 13:15-16** Good understanding giveth favour: But the way of transgressors is hard. Every prudent man dealeth with knowledge: But a fool layeth open his folly. Why do I say it is easy? If we endeavor to do only what God says to do, everything we do will prosper. Psalm 1:3 And he shall be like a tree planted by the rivers of water, that bringeth forth his fruit in his season; his leaf also shall not wither; and whatsoever he doeth shall prosper.

So, we will not ask God what to wear to work tomorrow but we will consult His word about Godly attire. We will not ask God what's for dinner, but we will consult God's word about what foods are good for the body that He created. We will not ask God if this man is who we should marry but we will consult God's word about the characteristics of a God-fearing man. This is how you live in His will. You develop an appetite for reading and consulting His word because His word is

His will. Proverbs 3:6 - In all thy ways acknowledge him, and he shall direct thy paths. I heard you. You just said, "Lord I need a do-over!" Smile. Well, Thank God He is in the do-over business! Mastering being alone with God and His creation happened before God created help for Adam. Just as Adam learned to live with, name and co-exist with God's creation, so must we. We were born into a world full of God's creation. Other people were already here when we got here. If we failed at relationships with the people in our own environments, it is safe to assume that we will fail with any other relationships we may form.

Learning to live in peace and balance in every environment is the goal. There is biblical help. Hebrews 12:14 Follow peace with all men, and holiness, without which no man shall see the Lord: Proverbs 15:1 A soft answer turneth away wrath: but grievous words stir up anger. Philippians 2:2-4 Fulfil ye my joy, that ye be likeminded, having the same love, being of one accord, of one mind. Let nothing be done through strife or vainglory; but in lowliness of mind let each esteem other better than themselves. Look not every man on his own things, but every man also on the things of others.

Oh, I can do this all day. The common thread here is that the guideline for forming and maintaining lasting relationships with anyone on earth is found clearly delineated in the word of God.

Lesson Challenge

Challenge 2.1

What are some of life's circumstances that may have influenced you to lose focus on the will of

God for your life?

_____

_____

_____

_____

_____

_____

_____

_____

_____

_____

_____

_____

_____

_____

_____

_____

_____

_____

_____

_____

_____

_____

Challenge 2.2
When challenges arose in a relationship and you realized what you were getting was not what you desired, what are some of the ways you tried to get your will's desire to become a reality in your life? How did it work out?

_____

_____

_____

_____

_____

_____

_____

_____

_____

_____

_____

_____

_____

_____

_____

_____

_____

_____

_____

_____

_____

_____

Challenge 2.3

Have you ever felt like consulting the Bile about everything is unnecessary or unrealistic? If so, why?

_____

_____

_____

_____

_____

_____

_____

_____

_____

_____

_____

_____

_____

_____

_____

_____

_____

_____

_____

_____

_____

_____

_____

_____

Final Challenge
Do you believe that you can or should live your entire life according to the Bible?

_____

_____

_____

_____

_____

_____

_____

_____

_____

_____

_____

_____

_____

_____

_____

_____

_____

_____

_____

_____

_____

_____

LESSON THREE
Biblically Single – Naked and Not Ashamed

We must be taught to follow the guideline for being biblically single, then married. For single women who are born-again, this is much easier than it would be for those who are already married according to the custom of this world and or according to the will of the flesh, but it is not impossible. Before marriage, a single or unmarried woman's desire should be consistent with the will of God for her life. She should accept that she has never been alone and that it is not natural for her to be alone, and she must be satisfied with Christ as her other self until such time as she is married.

This sounds like a fairytale in our day and age. I can almost hear the sneering and the nodding of heads, but my prayer is that this very biblical concept resonates into the heart of at least one single (unmarried) woman reading this book. I wish that I could write a book about the joy of single living! Oh, the shopping, partying, traveling, beauty secrets and off and on love affairs; except none of this is a part of the will of God for her life and that alone will not turn out well for a Believer in Jesus Christ. I've read that book to the end, and it does not end well. The real truth is that the only life that will satisfy the will of God is a life that is sinless and follows the simple biblical guideline for single living.

There is a single and there is a biblically single and a choice must be made. I have not yet touched the conversation about sex. When I refer to biblically single, I mean heart, mind, and soul. A mind that is determined to find and be in the will of God for life. That kind of mind leads to a kind of lifestyle and daily walk. Whether a person has already engaged in worldly, sexual activities or not, this mindset and lifestyle is attainable. It is not for bragging points or to be used as some form of spiritual superiority, it is simply because she is a believer in Jesus Christ and understands that life is better when it is lived in alignment with God's will.

You will see single women whose lives are drama filled. They must occupy every moment of their lives with entertainment, relationships, friends, social living, shopping, social media, and work. They are simply not satisfied unless they have found something to do with themselves. But a single, Godly woman's life is more like Eve's, simple. She is content to exist in this world without all of the drama. She likes to look nice but is not manic about her appearance. Her hair and skin are beautiful as she likes it. She looks in the mirror and loves who she sees. She is grateful and says, I will praise thee; for I am fearfully and wonderfully made: marvelous are thy works; and that my soul knoweth right well! Her body type is her body type. She is careful not to put anything into her body that will upset her natural rhythm. She sees her body as the temple of the living God and is determined to take care of it as she would God's temple. She is naked – stripped of the cares of this world - and not ashamed.

She is only concerned with having friends who are like-minded and her social media life is limited to edifying, uplifting content. Her delight is in the law of the Lord and in His law does she but his delight is in the law of the Lord; **and** in his law doth (s)he **meditate day and night.** She is able to live in this world but not be of this world and she is perfectly content with that. She has no need or desire to cry aloud, spare not or lift up her voice against sin, only in her own life. She is not angry with sinners, nor does she show that she is secretly desirous of anyone else's life. When asked, she will share her life's convictions with others and by obligation and love for Jesus Christ, she will endeavor to make disciples and carry out the great commission.

Whatever she needs, she will pray to the Father. Whatever she desires, she will pray to the Father. Whenever she is weak, she will pray to the Father and because she pleases Him, no request will be denied. She is content to wait on the Lord and while waiting she will be of good courage and the Lord with strengthen her heart to wait for his perfect timing. This is peace. This is prosperity. This is contentment and godliness. This is being biblically single.

Because of her lifestyle and her stance, only a certain type of man will choose her. This is the type of man she desires. She does not ever think that she must add to herself in order to get a man to desire her. She will never entertain an idea of showing her sexiness, her curves, or her cleavage to attract a man. The man she seeks is more like Adam, a man who is satisfied to do the will of God for his life and seeks a woman who is suitable for him to do that and less like someone who seeks a woman to put on display as he does his beautiful timepiece. Because she lives it, she will easily recognize it and can spot a perpetrator a mile away. She knows who she is and whose she is. She knows that her Father knows what is best for her and if she acknowledges Him in all of her ways, He will direct her path. She will say yes to one, who like herself, is naked and not ashamed. I get it. The modern-day single woman is influenced by television shows like, Living Single, in a 90's kind of world, I'm glad I've got my girls! Ministry has changed and if you're not a colored-up Barbie type with a snatched, waist trained ribcage, you simply do not fit in. Single's ministry is more like the dating game. Lots of drama, very little ministry. Perhaps it should be called real-life stories of single or unmarried Christian women. Far be it from me to try to take away the fun and excitement of it all but the truth is, most of it is entertainment at best, with a little dare-to be different flavor. Let's talk about sex baby, how to pick the right one this time, do-you-boo and self-care. It's all good, but it's not ministry. Ministry focuses on biblical truth and the life of the biblically single. It's not bad, it's just not biblical. Biblical is boring but it is exactly what is needed to end the cycles of marriage by trial and error.

The previous description of Eve as the woman who is content with the role of help suitable for her man makes her look like a totally boring Stepford wife or a boring housewife with no life of her own, no mind, no ideas, no business, no respect. Most women of this day and age would never aspire to that, including me. However, it is the innocence of being satisfied with being in the will of God that I am trying to emphasize. The Eve of the garden was not the same Eve of the 21st century but we can get back to Eden in our mentality and spirituality. We should live our lives in such a way that God's will is prioritized over our own.

If the single life was not biblical and the choice for a husband is not biblical, the marriage will not be biblical. The wedding might be spectacular, the sex might be amazing, and the friendship might be perfect, but the great divide will happen at the place of biblical conviction. At some point the wife must be suitable for the man to do the will of God for his life. Marrying a man who could care less about the will of God for his life is a disaster waiting to happen. There. I said it.

Are there not good men, who live morally decent lives, are good providers and great husbands? Of course, there are! But once a woman becomes a disciple of Jesus Christ, it is her duty to make a disciple out of that good man, whether she is married to him or not. The yoke of relationships must be borne equally or there will be tension at the neck. If this good man is a good man but unwilling to become a disciple of Jesus Christ and committed to living his life according to the word of God, there will be unequivocal tension in that area.

Genesis 2:18 "And the Lord God said, It is not good that the man should be alone; I will make him an help meet for him." Genesis 2:18 The all-familiar story begins with the very reason for our existence ladies. After God masterfully designed and crafted his most precious commodity, in whom he breathed his very own breath and man became a living soul, he said, "It is NOT good." For the first time in the history of His creative utterances we hear the negative. After having said that everything He created was good, we hear the strange utterance of negativity out of the mouth of God. "It is not good that the man should be alone."

Lesson Challenge

Challenge 3.1
What kind of *single* are/were you? How is that working or how has that worked for you?

_____

_____

_____

_____

_____

_____

_____

_____

_____

_____

_____

_____

_____

_____

_____

_____

_____

_____

_____

_____

_____

_____

_____

Challenge 3.2

Have you noticed any repeating cycles in your life? If so, what are they and why do you think the cycle repeats?

_____

_____

_____

_____

_____

_____

_____

_____

_____

_____

_____

_____

_____

_____

_____

_____

_____

_____

_____

_____

_____

Challenge 3.3
What do you think may be the reason(s) you are single if not by choice?

_____

_____

_____

_____

_____

_____

_____

_____

_____

_____

_____

_____

_____

_____

_____

_____

_____

_____

_____

_____

_____

_____

_____

_____

_____

_____

_____

_____

_____

_____

Final Challenge

If God gave you a specific and guaranteed guideline for how to go from single to married what are some of the questions you should ask before starting?

_____

_____

_____

_____

_____

_____

_____

_____

_____

_____

_____

_____

_____

_____

_____

_____

_____

_____

_____

_____

_____

_____

_____

LESSON FOUR

The Game of Thrones: Spiritual Warfare for the Family

After mankind sinned in the garden, they became conscious of everything and commenced to hiding from God. In this instance, hiding from a God you know to be omniscient is in fact hiding from truth. They needed God. They wanted to stay in the presence of God, but they were not yet able to handle the truth they desired.

Of all the millions of trees at their disposal, they decided to choose the one that God had forbidden. This is an interesting thought about human nature that once we know it, we can use it to avoid some very possible pitfalls and disasters. We are naturally prone to the forbidden and that is why God had to give them specific instructions. His word does the same thing today. It warns us to avoid the forbidden. It must be a deliberate and conscious action on our part to stay away from what we have been told by God to avoid. Adam and Eve's failure to do so, caused a life-long cycle of regrets.

Adam and Eve were the progenitors of the first family and from day one, Satan was against it. Let us pay close attention to this very well-calculated plan of attack against the family to be sure that we are not victims or partakers in what we cannot readily see with our natural eyes. Adam and Eve were tempted to *open their eyes* but their disobedience actually closed their eyes to the splendor of their relationship with God, the creator of the world, to the perfection of the Garden of delight in which they lived freely and most importantly, to the deceit in the hand that offered them the option! Let me remind you again about their purpose for creation. *Be fruitful and multiply. Replenish the earth and subdue it.*

Satan understood the power of their unity to be enough to subdue the earth and take dominion of it; dominion that he wanted for himself. Their sin gave him exactly what he wanted. This book is written to keep as many as read it from making the very same mistake in our current day. Yes! It is a tool, a weapon that reveals the subtlety of Satan, particularly against unity. The union of marriage is honorable unto God and therefore deplorable to Satan. The united family is a threat to his dominion. He cannot wreak havoc from generation to generation in a family that is equally yoked together in God's word. A unified church is a threat to his spiritual dominion in the lives of church-going Believers. Let's get at it!

Just as blessings are transferable from generations to generations, so must be the opposite. Curses and specific demonic attacks are targeted at specific families for reasons unknown to them. Because these are spiritual attacks that are orchestrated in the spirit-realm it will take spiritual revelation to identify them. We are taught to war in the flesh, but very few of us are taught to do spiritual warfare; this leaves us ill-equipped to combat the attacks of an unseen enemy. Even those who are of the faith may find themselves failing and being defeated because we are attempting to fight a spiritual battle in the flesh or carnally. This is the reason there is no peace at home, in the marriage and/or in the family. Romans 8:6 In-Context 6 For to be carnally minded is death; but to be spiritually minded is life and peace. 7 Because the carnal mind is enmity against God: for it is not subject to the law of God, neither indeed can be.

For those who dare to continue this journey with me, not only will you learn the secrets of specific spiritual warfare for the family, we will go into the darkness for your family in intercessory prayer and do warfare in the spirit with you and for you. This will be a short victory because our enemy has already been defeated. No longer will we travail and spend hours in warfare! Luke 10:19 assures us that we have what it takes and that our enemy has been defeated at calvary.

There are many of reasons that families are targeted, reasons that clearly go as far back as Genesis with the deception of the first family and carried on throughout slavery, when the first thing any captor did was change the "sir-name" or family name of a slave. The family name is a representation of ownership and culture. In ancient Babylon, Nebuchadnezzar ordered their Jewish captor's names to be changed to assimilate them into Babylonian culture: "Daniel to Belteshazzar, Hananiah to Shadrach, Mishael to Meshach, and Azariah to Abednego." (Daniel 1:7)

When Satan wants or needs to own an entire family, he targets the family. If that family name is targeted, the demonic order continues from generation to generation. You will notice how certain destructive traits seem to go from one generation to the next in certain families. While we don't always know why - we can be assured of what. Satanic infiltration is always a game of thrones! A war for territory and occupancy. It is the same motive now as it was in the garden, to take away man's dominion.

While we can easily tie family illnesses and family similarities to lifestyle, decisions and eating habits together; these are natural and carnal, but we are not only flesh and blood, we are also spirit and must be careful to root out anything that attaches itself to us spiritually. It's like only taking care of the outside of our bodies and ignoring the inside. Regular cleansing and detoxing must happen on the inside to keep the body functioning as it is intended. Now, God has made the body to do this without any assistance when we put the right things into our bodies. With fast food, fake foods, and a world full of products unrecognizable to our natural body's systems, regular natural detoxification is difficult and most times not possible.

Our spirits are also tainted with unrecognizable foods and substances that prohibit it from self-regulation. It is God's word that is able to identify and root out foreign substances attached to our spirit. Jesus says John 6:63 KJV It is the spirit that quickeneth; the flesh profiteth nothing: the words that I speak unto you, they are spirit, and they are life. If our life is not regulated by God's word, it is regulated by the flesh alone. God forbid!

The analogy god gave me for that is of a bed bug infestation. The bedbug is invisible to the naked eye, but the effects of infestation are very visible. The characteristics of bedbugs are the following:

- Tiny and virtually invisible to the naked eye: **Satan** is a personal, **spiritual** being who rebelled against God and leads a **spiritual** kingdom composed of demonic powers who oppose God's purposes.
- Fast-breeding - seeking whom he may devour. **1 Peter 5:8**

- Needs blood to survive - Satan needs access: **1 Peter 5:8** Be sober-minded; be watchful. Your adversary the devil prowls around like a roaring lion, seeking whom he may devour.

- Causes irritation - we respond differently when we are irritated or vexed - Matthew 15:22 And, behold, a woman of Canaan came out of the same coasts, and cried unto him, saying, Have mercy on me, O Lord, *thou* Son of David; my daughter is **grievously vexed** with a devil.

- Attacks in the dark - once the lights are turned on, they hide - they do not leave they hide! The house is clean but they are still there, just hidden. **Ephesians 6:12** For we wrestle not against flesh and blood, but against principalities, against powers, **against the rulers of the darkness** of this world, against spiritual wickedness in high places. **Acts 26:18a** to open their eyes, and to turn them from darkness to light, and from the power of Satan unto God

- Attacks while people are at rest: **Matt. 13:25** but while men slept, his enemy came and sowed tares among the wheat and went his way. **Amos 6:6** Woe to them that are at ease in Zion, and trust in the mountain of Samaria, which are named chief of the nations, to whom the house of Israel came!

Our first response is to blame someone. Who let it in? Where did it come from? What is it attached to? Throw away everything! - these are common questions but are almost impossible to answer with certainty. Throwing out the bed does nothing if the infestation is in the flooring or the walls! So, someone has to invest the money and time in hiring a professional to bring in a steamy substance - why steam? Because gas - extreme heat or extreme cold - gets into all of the crevices and infiltrates the nests and the mother-breeder is destroyed!

What's happening in most families is the blame game, the confusion, and the throwing away of what we think is infested. But the truth is we need the Holy Spirit to infiltrate the crevices and get down into the root of the problem! **1 Corinthians 2:10** But God hath revealed them unto us by his Spirit: for the Spirit **searcheth all things, yea, the deep things of God. This is the essence of Spiritual Warfare!**

Let's talk about those foreign substances or devices that attach themselves to our spirits and ultimately wreak havoc on our families from generation to generation and why.

- **Addiction:** Substances, gambling, and Sexual Perversion" Addictions destroy families
- **Sexual Perversion:** Pornography and Homosexuality - Gender confusion: Sexual pleasure without procreation. Fornication and Adultery/infidelity: Sexual pleasure without intentional procreation. If procreation happens, the family is divided.
- **Sickness/ Disease:** Shortened lifespan and ultimate destruction of the family
- **Anger/Rage:** Destruction of family - incarceration - separation of family
- **Inconsistency:** Double-mindedness blocks the blessings of the family

Lesson Challenge

Challenge 4.1

What are some possible demonic devices that may have been devised against your family, past or present?

_____

_____

_____

_____

_____

_____

_____

_____

_____

_____

_____

_____

_____

_____

_____

_____

_____

_____

_____

_____

_____

_____

_____

Challenge 4.2

Have you been victim to or a progenitor of any possible demonic devices that may have been formed against your family?

_____

_____

_____

_____

_____

_____

_____

_____

_____

_____

_____

_____

_____

_____

_____

_____

_____

_____

_____

_____

_____

_____

Challenge 4.3

What do you think may be the reason(s) your family may have been targeted by Satan?

Final Challenge
What are some things you can do to cancel an assigned attack against the prosperity of your family or someone else's family that may be targeted by Satan?

_____

_____

_____

_____

_____

_____

_____

_____

_____

_____

_____

_____

_____

_____

_____

_____

_____

_____

_____

_____

_____

_____

LESSON FIVE
The Basket-Case Baptism

Warning. This will be a baptism for some. I'm going hard on this baptism, and it may cause a little heat to rise under some of our collars but let me remind you of the difference between the two biblical baptisms. One is water baptism and the second baptism that is mentioned in the Bible is the Baptism of the Holy Spirit-*and with fire*. The Baptism of the Holy Spirit is representative of the burning up of sin in the inward person, thus giving opportunity for new life in the spirit. The great difference in the baptisms is one buries and the other burns. Let us endeavor to remain focused on the desired outcome ... opportunity for new, as opposed to the burning up of sin.

The most effective tool of the enemy against mankind is carnality, the will of the flesh. The carrying case for that tool for women is our emotions. We have been referred to as emotional basket-cases for generations, but I dare not say that it is because we carry a plethora of emotions, because everyone has emotions- but perhaps it is because we carry *the carnal mind,* the most effective tool of the enemy in our baskets, and those baskets are interwoven with a plethora of emotions. Slow down and read it again.

Yup! I'm coming for that flesh.

The first thing we are going to baptize is self-centeredness, selfishness or what I sometimes call, *me-ism.* We must be able to admit and be willing to bury any semblance of selfish thoughts or ideas. We must be willing to denounce any ideas of self over others and reevaluate terms like, self-love, self-preservation, self-worth, self-esteem, and self-preservation. While all of these are real terms with real meaning, we must be willing to baptize all of them and come up with a new mindset about it all. Remember baptism is the going down of one and the coming up of a newer, more effective mind-set. This can only happen with the revelation of God's word.

What does the Bible say about how we should view ourselves?

- *"So, God created mankind in his own image, in the image of God he created them; male and female he created them"* (**Genesis 1:27**.)

- *"Yet to all who did receive him, to those who believed in his name, he gave the right to become children of God"* (**John 1:12**.)

- *You are altogether beautiful, my darling; there is no flaw in you"* (**Song of Solomon 4:7**.)

- *"God made him who had no sin to be sin for us, so that in him we might become the righteousness of God"* (**2 Corinthians 5:21**.)

- *I will praise thee; for I am fearfully and wonderfully made: marvelous are thy works; and that my soul knoweth right well. (**Psalm 139:14**)*

In essence, we should see ourselves as God sees us. Most of us have no problem seeing ourselves in a positive light and for those of us who do not, we simply need to read and believe what God says about us in his word. Yet so many of us are running from conference to conference trying to increase our esteem of ourselves. I get it and I am all for maximizing our self-esteem, but the challenge happens when we make esteem of ourselves more valuable than esteem of others.

What do we make of Philippians 2:3-4 "Do **nothing** out of selfish ambition or vain conceit. Rather, in humility value others above yourselves, not looking to your own interests but each of you to the interests of the others." This verse alone represents the entire baptism of self. The keyword, *nothing* means exactly what it says. While we generally have no problem doing things for others, many of us need to re-examine our motives.

Doing things or giving services with selfish motives is equal to doing nothing. One of the biggest traps we fall victim to is doing things or performing services while wanting recompence or rewards for doing them. It's what I call an *idiot trap* because we are often trying to convince ourselves and others that we want nothing in return.

If you are contracted to do a service for a fee, this is called business. If you are kind to people and expect that your kindness to them merits kindness from them, you are stuck in an *idiot trap* because in most cases it never comes back from them in the exact proportion that it was given.

Marriages, relationships, and commitments are failing because of this invisible trap. We all want things. We all want love. We all wanted to be treated well. We all want to be respected and it is true to Scripture that in order to get these things from people, we must first be willing to give them. An example of that is Proverbs 18:24, **A man** that hath **friends must** shew **himself friendly**: and there is a friend that sticketh closer than a brother. The problem with this exists when we expect the return to come from those to whom we give it. It is very possible to show yourself friendly to someone who does not return friendship to you. Does this mean that you should cease to show yourself friendly? Of course not. Galatians 6:7 says Be not deceived; God is not mocked: for whatsoever a man soweth, that shall he also reap. This guarantees that you will reap what you sow but it never guarantees that you will reap from the place or person to whom you have sown.

Wives who are frustrated because over time, she believes that she is the only one giving in a relationship or is hurt and broken because the love, time, respect, sacrifice and/or affection she is giving to her spouse is not being returned to her from him are the reasons for this book. No one can say that this would not be very painful to handle but the first thing we must realize is whether these allegations are real and not imagined, whether they are facts and not just feelings. Many of us are content to believe that if we feel it or if we think it, it is a fact. We have a long list of evidence to prove our theories and it is often hard, if not impossible, to prove them otherwise. Today I will offer those women a fresh new set of eyes and an opportunity for redirection. This is not to say that every person who feels this way is not absolutely right, but first, I believe it is important to know for sure before we draw any conclusions and/or make any decisions for how to proceed. Fair? Please know that I feel your pain. I have personally been there and thought that life would stay that way for me. I did not think it could possibly get worse. Thank God he loves his daughters. I was once privy to a seat at someone's table who would tell me the painful but healing truth and start the process of lifetime change for me.

Lesson Challenge

Challenge 5.1

Describe a seriously painful offense you have experienced recently without using any pronouns except me or I. Use no references to *the person* and call no one's name except your own. Was this possible? Was this difficult? Would you like to share?

_____

_____

_____

_____

_____

_____

_____

_____

_____

_____

_____

_____

_____

_____

_____

_____

_____

_____

_____

_____

_____

_____

Challenge 5.2

What were you feeling afterward? Notice, I did not say how did *that or it –* (both pronouns) make you feel. This is because feelings are chosen, not forced.

_____

_____

_____

_____

_____

_____

_____

_____

_____

_____

_____

_____

_____

_____

_____

_____

_____

_____

_____

_____

_____

Challenge 5.3
What did you learn from your feeling(s) – Nothing is an acceptable answer.

_____

_____

_____

_____

_____

_____

_____

_____

_____

_____

_____

_____

_____

_____

_____

_____

_____

_____

_____

_____

_____

_____

_____

Challenge 5.4
What decision(s) did you make afterward? Why?

_____

_____

_____

_____

_____

_____

_____

_____

_____

_____

_____

_____

_____

_____

_____

_____

_____

_____

_____

_____

_____

_____

_____

_____

Final Challenge
If you made any decision at all, did it benefit you? If so, how?

_____

_____

_____

_____

_____

_____

_____

_____

_____

_____

_____

_____

_____

_____

_____

_____

_____

_____

_____

_____

_____

_____

_____

LESSON SIX
Misguided Perception

I will begin by sharing a chapter from a book I wrote called, Redirection some years ago with women like you in mind. It is called **MISGUIDED PERCEPTION.**

I have chosen to throw myself under the bus in this work as a sacrifice for the betterment of others. Thank me later. When I got married nearly 28 years ago, I never said it or even thought of it, but I learned later that I really wanted to be the perfect wife. I just wanted to do everything right. You may or may not know, but not being right was a big problem for me. Needless for me to say, I was wrong … a lot. In this chapter I will share some of the misguided perceptions I had as a wife. (God help me!)

First of all, it was misguided to think I could be the perfect wife with no training, no experience, and no personal mentors. It was also misguided for me to think that my new husband expected me to be the perfect wife, although it felt that way after every mistake I made.

Day after day I found myself trying to prove one thing or the other. I didn't know then that I was trying to prove things, but I found out later. I would break into fits of anger when I believed I was falsely accused. I did not use any spiritual discernment. In my mind, my marriage was not Kingdom it was just my marriage and I had to make it work. Big mistake!

Christian marriage is called Holy Matrimony; it is done in a church and sanctioned by a minister. When asked, "What should be different about a Christian Marriage?" Gotquestions.org says this, "The primary difference between a Christian marriage and a non-Christian marriage is that Christ is the center of the marriage. When two people are united in Christ, their goal is to grow in Christlikeness throughout the life of the marriage. Non-Christians may have goals for their marriage, but *Christlikeness* is not one of them. This is not to say that all Christians, when they marry, immediately begin to work toward this goal. Many young Christians don't even realize this is actually the goal, but the presence of the Holy Spirit within each of them works with them, maturing each one so that the goal of Christlikeness becomes increasingly clear to them."

Our case was very similar except we were both pretty seasoned Christians; we were both filled with the Holy Spirit and we were both well versed in the Scripture. You would think we would never, ever have a fight. Not!

Neither of us thought of the goal of our marriage as growing in Christlikeness throughout the life of the marriage. We had a misguided perception about the main goal. We knew we would both love God and serve God, but we were not using our marriage to do that.

We made spiritual plans to serve in ministry together, to love each other, to have a family, to work together financially, to establish a home and perhaps a business. We assumed that we were already Christlike and, for the most part, we were but there is nothing like marriage to show you where you are not!

Our first really heated argument began with us trying to determine who was more effective in the Civil Rights Movement, Martin Luther King, or Malcom X. Why did I say Malcom X when Martin Luther King was a Christian and practiced non-violence? How could I, as a Christian, possibly believe that Malcom X was more effective?

Well, I cannot even remember what my reasons were then, and they do not matter much now. What matters most is that the argument was more about a challenge of my Christlikeness than my civil rights opinion. Some of our fiercest fights were challenges to each other's Christian character. Most arguments would end up with statements like, "And you're supposed to be saved!"

The misguided idea that Christians cannot make mistakes in judgment and still be Christians can cause serious harm to meaningful relationships. There are entire Christian reformations and churches that do not fellowship with one another because one is right, and the other is wrong.

Redirection to the Cross of Calvary should ease the pain but that is a conversation for another day.

While I cannot speak for my husband or his thought processes around those dark seasons, I can certainly speak to mine. So many times, he would say one thing and I would hear something totally different. I confess that I may have had misguided perceptions that caused or exacerbated serious but unnecessary fights and arguments. Thank you for asking, I will share.

When my husband expressed his dislike for something I did or said, I would jump quickly to my own defense. He would say, "I don't like *it*" but I would hear, "*I don't like you*" in hindsight, I can hear myself saying over and over, "Maybe you should go find the kind of wife you really want." My perception was that he just didn't like *me*. I responded every single time with that perception, and I realize now that I was trying, for many years, to prove that I was right about that perception. It was self-destructive. It was the reason I did not have lasting relationships. I would believe that my lack of perfection caused people to dislike me and I was determined to prove it. How dumb is that? It was my reality. My misguided perception that everyone expected me to do everything right and if I didn't, they would no longer care for me was a big mistake. It was quite grand of me to think anyone even thought I could be perfect.

I worked the overnight shift at Dow Jones, Inc. and I had abused my Black-Car privilege by taking black cars to church services on my lunch break. My heart was right, but my work ethic was poor. It turned out that the company found out, of course, and my supervisor called me in. Instead of owning up to my mistake in judgment, agreeing to pay the bills in an attempt to keep a great job, I quit. I left a resignation letter under his door during the night shift. This was a terrible mistake. I perceived that he was going to fire me anyway and was too proud to be humiliated, especially being a Christian. I found out later that he had no intention of firing me and had in fact done the same thing a time or two. He was ready to forgive all with a slap on the wrist but, like a fool, I had already quit.

This is the same young woman who used to think that her pastor, *"just didn't like her"* so she rebelled over, and over trying to prove her misguided perception. It is not until we have people in our lives who are determined to love us regardless of our misguided perceptions that we will have lasting relationships. It is precisely why Jesus could say on the cross, *"Father, forgive them for they know not what they do."* They are misguided in their perceptions about me, but they are worth saving.

If I had known then what I know now, I would have tried to see things from another perspective. I would have tried to *hear* better. I would have tried to understand things from a biblical perspective and not from my emotions and my feelings. If I had been as close to God as I thought I was, I am sure I would have handled things more spiritually maturely. I am grateful that God, my pastor and my husband were determined to love me regardless of my misguided perceptions. I thank God for *time*.

There are other misguided perceptions that work directly against marriages. Perceptions about infidelity, insecurity, intentions, and mindsets can make or break a good marriage. This makes it more and more quintessential for Christian couples to work together in prayer and study. Holiness and righteous living make the Christian marriage complete. *"Righteousness exalteth a nation; but sin is a reproach to any people"* Proverbs 14:34

I cannot leave here without addressing the invisible elephant in the room, *Competition*. Couple after couple have come into the office for counseling and each with a fierce determination to prove who is the better mate. One may come in earlier or seek private consultation to paint the other in a very poor light. This is an effort to bring bias to the opinion of the counselor at the on-set. Everyone wants to be right. Everyone wants to be the one with the better judgment and everyone wants justification for their actions. Very few come into counseling with a sincere desire to *fix this*.

Oh, I know it quite well. It is not until things have reached the point of devastation that people like her yearn for a resolve. In the heat of the battle there is a fierce competition going on between the better spouse, the better Christian, the better parent and ultimately the better person. Both want the counselor to choose them but here lies the fundamental concept that is so big it cannot be seen; it is the inability to see the forest for the trees … they chose each other! The husband has chosen the wife as the best choice for his marriage and the wife has chosen the husband as the best choice for her marriage! The counselor will never be able to choose who is the better person when both are the best persons for each other. Got it?

The counselor's best option is to show these two how they are better together than they are apart. He must show them concepts and ways to work through any dilemma *together.* He must effectively redirect their drama to the greater good for them, *together.* When divorce is not an option for a Kingdom couple, redirection is the key! A wise counselor will allow this couple to expose both perceptions to each other and then offer another, more beneficial, more provable perception and that will have to come from the wisdom of God.

For example, a couple who is having a major fall-out about a co-parenting issue may bring out all of the faults perceived about each other without once addressing it from the child or children's perception. What is this doing to the child? Once this couple is able to see this situation from another perception then there is hope for a resolve. How can we work together to resolve this dilemma with the best outcomes for *all* involved? A wise counselor will be able to help here.

King Solomon faced a more devastating but similar dilemma. In 1 Kings 3:16–28 we find an account of King Solomon hearing a case involving two prostitutes. The two women had both recently given birth to sons, and they lived together in the same home. During the night, one of the infants was smothered and died. The woman whose son had died switched her dead baby with the baby of the other woman as she slept. The other woman, seeking justice, took the matter before the king. She stated her case: "We were alone; there was no one in the house but the two of us. During the night this woman's son died because she lay on him. So, she got up in the middle of the night and took my son from my side while I, your servant, was asleep. She put him by her breast and put her dead son by my breast. The next morning, I got up to nurse my son—and he was dead! But when I looked at him closely in the morning light, I saw that it wasn't the son I had borne" (verses 18–21). Solomon could not tell from their words which woman was telling the truth. Instead, he issued a shocking command: *"Bring me a sword. . .. Cut the living child in two and give half to one and half to the other"* (1 Kings 3:24–25). After he said this, the woman whose son was still alive said, "Please, my lord, give her the living baby! Don't kill him!" However, the other woman, whose son had died, answered, "Neither I nor you shall have him. Cut him in two!" (verse 26). Based on their responses, Solomon knew the identity of the true mother: "Give the living baby to the first woman. Do not kill him; she is his mother" (verse 27). Why would Solomon give such an outrageous command? Did he really intend to cut a baby in half with a sword? The text is clear that Solomon's intention was to discover the truth. He did so by watching the responses of the two women and relying on the maternal instincts of the true mother. (https://www.gotquestions.org/Solomon-two-prostitutes.html)

King Solomon used the wisdom of God to redirect the mothers' thinking from themselves to the life of the child. His suggestion to cut the child in half changed their perceptions about the situation. As long as the child was alive the liar would continue to lie but the concept of a dead child brought out the truth. The wisdom of God can challenge stubborn perceptions and get down to the truth. It is not until we deal in truth, absolute truth that we can get a lasting resolve and a better outcome.

What about a couple whose marriage has simply lost its luster? The light has gone out in both of their eyes for each other. It's over. A wise counselor must redirect them back to the days when there was luster and when the lights were burning brightly and then walk them patiently through the events that happened since then. I guarantee you that somewhere along that walk they will run into a misguided perception. One that screams, "I did not think that!" "I never said that!" "I did not mean that" or "It was not like that".

Again, I will put myself out there. Thank me later. One of the most trying seasons of my marriage, when I actually took a trip down south to "breathe" was entangled by a totally misguided perception. I was always on the defense about not being wanted. So much so that not being wanted was one of two things I considered to be grounds for divorce! I would not be in a marriage where I was unwanted or unloved. I would not try to make anyone *want* me. I was always on the lookout for it and most of my rages ended in, "Well, go and get the kind of woman you really want!" I told you earlier that when he said or showed that he did not like some*thing* I did or said, I took it to mean that he didn't like me. It is self-destructive in its nature. A self-fulfilling prophecy. I thought it, I knew it and I was determined to be right about it. I was preparing myself for an ultimate, inevitable break up that was completely unfounded. It was a misguided perception but if I continued in that vein and continued to respond to my own emotional perceptions, our marriage would not have stood a chance. This is the reason I am transparently sharing with you at the risk of you calling me all kinds of names.

I remember coming back and trying to explain to my husband that I did not feel his love for me; I did not see love in his eyes when he looked at me; I saw only disgust. The only conversations we had were complaints about one thing or another; what the members said about me, what he said about me and what I just did not do right. Perhaps we had gotten so busy being busy that what we once had faded away and this was what we were left with. Oh, yes! My argument was real. I was emotionally distraught. I could not see anything else. I went on and on only to see in the eyes of my husband total confusion. He had no idea where all of that was coming from. Thank God he was wise enough not to dismiss it as nothingness or female drama. I think he knew that I really believed what I was saying and was ready to do something about it. He put his arms tightly around me and squeezed me. He reassured me that he loved me very much and that he was very much in love with me. He told me that I was the best thing in his world and that he could not imagine life without me.

While this was reassuring and may have some of you shedding tears, the truth is that it had *never* ceased to be truth. He had always felt that way. It never changed but my perception of it had changed. Circumstances, times, events, and misguided perceptions caused a truth to be distorted and even dismissed as non-existent.

It is true that maybe he had not said it enough. It's true that maybe we had gotten so involved in ministry that the demands on our time together had been a challenge. It's true that maybe I had become jealous of his time spent with the ministry and the people in the ministry. It's true that I may have been threatened by his time with others as better times than spent with me. It's true that taking care of the children, the house and the family brought some distance over time, and all of this created a misguided perception of his true feelings for me.

I can hear some of you who know me thinking right now, as confident as she seems, I didn't know she was so insecure. It's O.K., neither did I. But I have learned that insecurity and vulnerability are not always bad words. I did not have anything to prove to anybody. If I had been strong enough to admit to those emotions instead of making wild unfounded assumptions, I would have had less drama in my life.

Can I help you? If I had been strong enough to say, "Baby I really want you to stay here with me tonight. I'm lonely. I'm feeling really vulnerable and insecure right now. I need my man. I need to be held ..." (I'm sure you're getting it) Instead of saying, "Are you going out again? The kids are going to say they only see me in this family because you're gone all the time ... blah, blah blah" things would probably have been a lot better for us.

On one of my re-reads, I heard in my spirit, someone asking, what if this was not the case? What if I was openly vulnerable and expressed my fears, insecurities, challenges, and suspicions verbally and my spouse retorted unfavorably? What if that approach did not work? What if things got worse as a result of my vulnerability?

My answer to the voice in my spirit is ... truth. You must get to the real truth about where your relationship is and where both of you think it is going. You cannot fool yourself into believing something that is not truth, and he cannot respond to you in untruthfulness. The real question is do you still love each other and are you willing to work to bring back the luster of your marriage? Once we get a truthful yes from the two of you, then we can back track to find out what really went wrong and how we can begin the healing process. What will not work is a response that says, "I do not know if I am still in love and I do not know if I am willing to work at a resolve." That, in my opinion, is a cop-out and usually means, "No, no, and no!" Before you jump all over my head, hear this. The sentence is quite different when said this way, "At this juncture, the way I am feeling right now, I'm not sure if I still love this person or if I want to work at a resolve." Agreed? This gives the counselor some leverage and gives the couple the benefit of time and counseling, time and prayer, time and wisdom and time in truthful communication.

My stance has always been, if you're staying, I will help you stay but if you're leaving, I will help you leave, but you cannot be staying and leaving at the same time. Once a person has made up his or her mind to leave, he or she is already gone but once a person has made up his or her mind to stay, he or she may never leave. My book. My opinion. Let's stay friends.

In relationships, maturity factors play a key part. Immature people often say what they do not mean, have things to prove, play too much but eventually get to their truth. Great counselors do not spend too much time on unstable relationships, so, they will get some initial information about the couple and their relationship. The idea that most people do not seek counseling until things have completely spiraled out of order is a good thing because at least the counselor knows they're ready for change.

You may be reading this book while facing a major challenge in your relationship. I trust that it helps you begin the process of redirection! Changing perceptions for better outcomes. I pray that you become vulnerable enough to ask the right questions and strong enough to accept truthful answers. I pray that each reader takes a personal stance at redirection and not expect change from anyone else but themselves.

Lesson Challenge

Challenge 6.1
Describe a seriously painful offense you have experienced recently without using any pronouns except me or I. Use no references to *the person* and call no one's name except your own. Was this possible? Was this difficult? Would you like to share?

_____

_____

_____

_____

_____

_____

_____

_____

_____

_____

_____

_____

_____

_____

_____

_____

_____

_____

_____

_____

_____

_____

Challenge 6.2
What were you feeling afterward? Notice, I did not say how did *that or it* – *(*both pronouns) make you feel. This is because feelings are chosen, not forced.

_____

_____

_____

_____

_____

_____

_____

_____

_____

_____

_____

_____

_____

_____

_____

_____

_____

_____

_____

_____

_____

_____

Challenge 6.3
What did you learn from your feeling(s) – Nothing is an acceptable answer.

_____

_____

_____

_____

_____

_____

_____

_____

_____

_____

_____

_____

_____

_____

_____

_____

_____

_____

_____

_____

_____

_____

_____

_____

Challenge 6.4

What decision(s) did you make afterward? Why?

_____

_____

_____

_____

_____

_____

_____

_____

_____

_____

_____

_____

_____

_____

_____

_____

_____

_____

_____

_____

_____

_____

_____

_____

Final Challenge
If you made any decision at all, did it benefit you? If so, how?

_____

_____

_____

_____

_____

_____

_____

_____

_____

_____

_____

_____

_____

_____

_____

_____

_____

_____

_____

_____

_____

_____

_____

ADDITIONAL RESOURCE

SCAN THE CODE TO DOWNLOAD

LESSON SEVEN
Offense, Defense

Pain, suffering, humiliation, insults, rejection, ridicule, and disregard – all offenses - have a way of bringing out the protector in us when our self-esteem is low. When we do not esteem ourselves fairly, we tend to call upon one of our chief protectors, the offense, or the defense. We tend to answer every challenge defensively or offensively. Defensive refers to actions or strategies taken to protect oneself or one's group, while offensive refers to actions or strategies taken to attack or defeat the opposition. In sports and military, defensive strategies are employed to prevent the opposing team or army from scoring or advancing, while offensive strategies are used to attempt to score or gain ground.

If we are not careful when we are offended, and very often, even when we are not, our attitudes are set for either defense or offense and either way, no one gets to hurt us anymore! We will either defend ourselves from a possible attack or prepare to stop the attack from coming altogether.

By attempting to defend ourselves from offenses or ward them off in advance, we may begin to read more into every answer, every response, and every action. Very often when we try to control the narratives in our lives, we may make enemies out of friends, and we may make a bad situation worse. The truth is, the only thing we can control is our response to the narrative.

A better use of our time is to work on our ability or disability to manage our emotions without the help of the offense or the defense. When we practice doing our best because we want the best outcomes, even if we do not get the desired outcome, we are assured that we have done our best. We are open to trying new ways, again and again, and to giving every try our very best effort. Maturity teaches us that we cannot control how another person behaves, not even with the best manipulation tactics, some may still surprise us. To do kind things with an expectation that the person we did it for would be grateful or pleased is normal but to do those things *so that* the person would be grateful or pleased is manipulation. This means that their response is what you want in return and in essence, the act of kindness was for you and not them. The difference is that when you genuinely do something to make a person happy, your posture is sad when they are not happy, you want to know what you can do to make it better. However, when you did an act of kindness so that the person could be happy, and your posture is mad that they did not reward you with their happiness after all of the effort you went through to make them happy, this was for you. You are not interested in doing anything else, instead you spend hours on the defense trying to make them understand why this thing should have made them happy. I hope this is making sense. For example, if you cook me food that you enjoy and expect me to enjoy it as much as you did, you would be more satisfied that I faked my enjoyment of the meal than for me to tell you that I did not enjoy the meal because making the meal was more for you than it was for me.

The best resolve is to ask me what I want, learn how I like it and make it for me because you want me to have it. Whether I eat it right away or change my mind and put it in the refrigerator for tomorrow, as long as you did your best, that is all.

Understanding and accepting that you cannot control a person's response or behavior and that your responsibility is only to control your own is a major victory in any relationship. Rebuking manipulation on any level is biblical. Being content with things as they are until they change is power. Content does not mean you do not want things to be better but it means you have exhausted all of your resources to make things better so you resolve to wait until you can or until someone else does. Learning to make the best of a bad situation without whining and complaining is maturity.

Babies jump up and down in the street when they cannot get what they want. They are using temper tantrums and crying in an attempt to control the parent's behavior. The parent cannot stop the child from screaming but must control their anger to avoid shaken baby syndrome or child abuse. They must control their emotions to stick with, "no means no."

The same applies to adults. Women who cry alone when they are hurt are obviously not using their tears as manipulation. The tears are natural responses to some emotional discomfort. Only God can understand the kind of pain that words cannot speak. Wise women go to God with challenges that their best efforts at communication cannot resolve. Wise women do not manipulate. Wise women do not attempt to control other people. Wise women are not intimidated by challenges. Wise women are flexible. Wise women do not compare themselves with anyone. Wise women are not too proud to change. Wise women are prepared for whatever comes next, even when they do not have a clue of what comes next. A wise woman prays until something happens no matter how long it takes. Proverbs 14:1 - Every wise woman buildeth her house: but the foolish plucketh it down with her hands.

GOALS:

Proverbs 31:10-31 Who can find a virtuous woman? for her price is far above rubies.

11 The heart of her husband doth safely trust in her, so that he shall have no need of spoil.

12 She will do him good and not evil all the days of her life.

13 She seeketh wool, and flax, and worketh willingly with her hands.

14 She is like the merchants' ships; she bringeth her food from afar.

15 She riseth also while it is yet night, and giveth meat to her household, and a portion to her maidens.

16 She considereth a field, and buyeth it: with the fruit of her hands she planteth a vineyard.

17 She girdeth her loins with strength, and strengtheneth her arms.

18 She perceiveth that her merchandise is good: her candle goeth not out by night.

19 She layeth her hands to the spindle, and her hands hold the distaff.

20 She stretcheth out her hand to the poor; yea, she reacheth forth her hands to the needy.

21 She is not afraid of the snow for her household: for all her household are clothed with scarlet.

22 She maketh herself coverings of tapestry; her clothing is silk and purple.

23 Her husband is known in the gates, when he sitteth among the elders of the land.

24 She maketh fine linen, and selleth it; and delivereth girdles unto the merchant.

25 Strength and honour are her clothing; and she shall rejoice in time to come.

²⁶ She openeth her mouth with wisdom; and in her tongue is the law of kindness.

²⁷ She looketh well to the ways of her household, and eateth not the bread of idleness.

²⁸ Her children arise up, and call her blessed; her husband also, and he praiseth her.

²⁹ Many daughters have done virtuously, but thou excellest them all.

³⁰ Favour is deceitful, and beauty is vain: but a woman that feareth the LORD, she shall be praised.

³¹ Give her of the fruit of her hands; and let her own works praise her in the gates.

You and I can be that wise woman, whether our husbands change or not. Whether our circumstances change or not. Whether our children, our jobs, our statuses, our finances, our health our bosses, our co-workers, our family members, our churches, our leadership etc. changes or not because we can only control our own responses.

FINAL NOTES

Question 1
What have I learned about myself during my time in this workbook?

_____

_____

_____

_____

_____

_____

_____

_____

_____

_____

_____

_____

_____

_____

_____

_____

_____

_____

_____

_____

_____

_____

_____

_____

Question 2
What am I prepared to change?

_____

_____

_____

_____

_____

_____

_____

_____

_____

_____

_____

_____

_____

_____

_____

_____

_____

_____

_____

_____

_____

_____

_____

_____

Question 3
What do I disagree with about this workbook? Why?

_____

_____

_____

_____

_____

_____

_____

_____

_____

_____

_____

_____

_____

_____

_____

_____

_____

_____

_____

_____

_____

_____

_____

Question 4
What are my present-day challenges and what am I now equipped to do about them?

_____

_____

_____

_____

_____

_____

_____

_____

_____

_____

_____

_____

_____

_____

_____

_____

_____

_____

_____

_____

_____

Question 5
What can I share from my life's experiences that will help others to become better?

_____

_____

_____

_____

_____

_____

_____

_____

_____

_____

_____

_____

_____

_____

_____

_____

_____

_____

_____

_____

_____

_____

_____

Question 6
What decisions have you made after completing this workbook?

_____

_____

_____

_____

_____

_____

_____

_____

_____

_____

_____

_____

_____

_____

_____

_____

_____

_____

_____

_____

_____

_____

Question 7

If you attended an accompanying Seat at My Table session, will you recommend it to other women and why or why not?

_____

_____

_____

_____

_____

_____

_____

_____

_____

_____

_____

_____

_____

_____

_____

_____

_____

_____

_____

_____

_____

_____

Question 8
What is your overall perception of this workbook and/or the accompanying session?

_____

_____

_____

_____

_____

_____

_____

_____

_____

_____

_____

_____

_____

_____

_____

_____

_____

_____

_____

_____

Made in the USA
Middletown, DE
24 September 2023

39268937R00044